symmetry

MARC J. STRAUS

TRIQUARTERLY BOOKS
NORTHWESTERN UNIVERSITY PRESS

EVANSTON, ILLINOIS

TriQuarterly Books
Northwestern University Press
Evanston, Illinois 60208-4210

Printed in the United States of America

ISBN 0-8101-5096-4 (cloth)
ISBN 0-8101-5097-2 (paper)

Library of Congress Cataloging-in-Publication Data

Straus, Marc J.
   Symmetry / Marc J. Straus.
     p. cm.
   ISBN 0-8101-5096-4 (cloth : alk. paper) — ISBN 0-8101-5097-2 (pbk.)
    1. Physician and patient—Poetry. 2. Physicians—Poetry. 3. Medicine—
Poetry. 4. Patients—Poetry. I. Title.

PS3569.T69213 S95 2000
811'.54—dc21

                              99-089019

for Livia Selmanowitz Straus

contents

*In both the contents and the text, an asterisk after a poem title indicates that the speaker of the poem is a patient.

acknowledgments

Grateful acknowledgment is made to the following journals and other publications in which some of the poems in this book were first published: *Controlled Burn* ("The Blue Hat"); *European Judaism* ("Chimes"); *Fan Magazine* ("Shoe Box"); *Hadassah Magazine* ("Chapel"); *Jewish Affairs* ("Green Dust"); *Journal of the American Medical Association* ("Before That," "Semaphore," "Words"); *Journal of the Medical Humanities* ("Breathing-Spoons," "Sunrise in Virgin Gorda," "Venetian Glass"); *Judaism* ("19332," "The Day Stalin Died," "My Father's Shadow"); *Kenyon Review* ("A Half Billion—More or Less," "Horseshoes"); *Mudfish* ("Fifth Finger," "Sand Crab"); *Passages North* ("Red Polka-Dot Dress"); *Pinyon Poetry* ("Butterfly"); *Ploughshares* ("Pinguid," "Sigh"); *Poetry East* ("Breathing Room" [published in this collection as "The Steam Bath"], "Not God," "The Rainy Season," "Say Yes"); *River Styx* ("Apple Cores"); *Tikkun* ("Le Mas du Luberon"); *TriQuarterly* ("Banner Hopes," "What I Am"); and *Virginia Quarterly Review* ("Like Me," "Over Roanoke," "Repetition").

"Before That" and "Semaphore" were reprinted in *Uncharted Lines: Poems from the Journal of the American Medical Association,* edited by Charlene Breedlove (Albany, Calif.: Boaz, 1998). "Chimes" was reprinted in "Lines off the Chart: A Doctor's Poems by Marc J. Straus," *Hadassah Magazine,* June/July 1999.

symmetry

I

Sand Crab

I walked along the bay
with my five-year-old nephew.
What are those little holes
with bubbles coming out?
he asked. Sand crabs, I said.
They hide under a thin layer
of sand to protect themselves.

Have you ever seen one?
he wanted to know. Yes,
I said, thinking of my first day
at the Washington V.A. Hospital.
A young man, age twenty-two,
was hidden under a white sheet.
He was pale as a moonbeam,

and his mouth puckered
in and out with each breath.
He had returned from Vietnam
with acute leukemia. His name
was Howard, I said
out loud. You're making
it up, my nephew laughed.

Red Polka-Dot Dress

I can't decide what to do,
her husband said, the X-ray films
still on the screen. He pulled out
a picture. This is us in 1963,
standing near the stone parapegm

built by the Greeks around 400 B.C.
On it they engraved the ruler's laws and
proclamations. That's Athena with
an eroded nose and worn-out hands.
Mildred's in a red polka-dot dress.

See how beautiful her auburn hair
looks in that morning light
pulled up in a bun above her neck.
And that's me holding her hand.
I see, I said.

Over Roanoke[*]

From thirty-three thousand feet
it looks like odd-shaped farms are pocketed
between deep green octopus hills,
pudgy tentacles coursing out.
Just yesterday the antibiotics were stopped.
One antifungal drug blistered
my mouth when the white count
dropped. I agree,
the smallest thing is loss of hair,
but the woman to my right
fidgets nervously. I want to say,
My eyebrows are bushy, the hair on my chest's
like baby silk . . .
The hills are folded up now
in long vertical ridges, and the few towns
are tucked alongside. I don't see how anyone
gets across.

Sigh*

I sighed this morning, a slow deep inspiration
that dragged the air into the recesses of my lungs,
portions I imagine had been forgotten
in the last few months. And then for a second
or two I felt the life pass out of me.
As if it were a prelude, a taste for the sake
of recognition, to diminish my anger.
As if it were a gift to make me more accepting,
so that when the angel lifts my hand
onto her atomless sleeve I will have no animosity.
She is so like my physician. He has no tolerance
for remonstration, his head is so cluttered
with obligatory data. I might articulate my pain
but he is filled with dying and I'm obliged
to keep the sigh inside.

Two Weeks*

A man's cough bounces down the hallway
like pick-up sticks. Three rooms away
an IV machine beeps constantly. I know
the distance by now. I know Mrs. Mandelkorn
was discharged today and Mr. Singer
died. Not just the overhead intercom blaring
Code Blue, or everyone running to his door.
It was the stillness afterward, the leaden walk
of the nurses. They've seen it before, but death fills
their shoes. They pass the pills in silence
and at the station their conversation is muted.
I asked Angela. She said he was old and frail
and his kidneys failed. It is more than
she should say, but she is kind
to differentiate his circumstance from mine.
I am here now two weeks.

Chapel*

There is a chapel downstairs. I passed it twice
on the way to radiology. No one was inside.
There are twelve wooden benches, a large crucifix
and stained glass above the altar. A note in the elevator says
"religious services for Jews available on request."
Today a priest came in and offered me absolution.
I think you have the wrong room, Father,
I said. He checked his notes, laughed courteously, and replied,
Now that I'm here. . . . A few minutes later I was sorry.
What harm is there to accept his prayer? I could borrow
his God for a while.

Before That

Synesthesia, metaplasia. Before that
my language was acquired on the corner of East Tenth Street,
Alice Singletary lip-synching every song, Archie
Grover starting every sentence with hey. Somehow
an occasional three-syllable word entered my vocabulary.
My tenth-grade paper was on Hemingway
and Mrs. Clara Mann wrote across the top in bold red
"needless to say you missed the symbolism entirely
in *A Farewell to Arms*—C minus." For the next exercise
she asked us to write a poem in class. I sat the hour
and angrily penned a dark and pessimistic verse. God
had disappeared in fear (and this was a religious school).
"This is an A plus," she wrote in red in the margin,
"but you must pay more attention to Yeats."
That may have been asking too much, but soon
I had found Rilke, Bishop, William Carlos
Williams, and Stanley Kunitz, who wrote about a slap
his mother gave him across the face when he was five
that still stung sixty years later. Words were pistols
and fireballs lined up like dominoes. Words
etched out the cilia in my throat and held my ankles down.
Later, in college and medical school, language stretched
on an unending yardarm. It became convoluted and specific.
Sometimes I yearned for simplicity—Joe Applebaum
tapping the top of a garbage can—do wop, do wop;
hey everybody, just do the hop.

The Blue Hat

The Doppler was negative, I said.
His son hugged him tightly

around the chest. I was about to say,
It would have been better if we had found

a clot. Now I suspected the cancer
had recurred. Outside, I could see

a yellow van. Its side lift lowered
and three people were taken out

in wheelchairs. One middle-aged man
with a blue wool hat was chattering constantly.

His left hand spiraled upward
in wide semicircles like swallows

starting south. I remembered the lecture
on hemiballismus. It was twenty-two years

ago and the professor mimicked
its motion. I continued to watch until

the movements stopped. For an instant
it seemed that a motionless hand

was holding the sky, then suddenly
it dropped, as if a bird had been shot.

Semaphore

Sometimes a word seems to fall
into an inaccessible gyrus
    of my brain and is lost forever.

Then there are times it snaps back,
coursing up from a hidden sulcus,
    bounding across thousands

of synapses. Adamantine recently
did that. It was a word I had once read
    and never looked up.

Then this week—brindled, gibbous,
Rift Valley fever, Gaucher's disease.
    In medical school I depended on

my excellent memory. I was quick.
I gathered them in, each word
    a shibboleth to be placed

in its proper quarry. Again today,
a patient I often see was in and
    I couldn't remember her name,

but then a girlfriend's phone number
from tenth grade came to mind.
    That's the proof. It's all there

carefully tucked away. Everything
is recoverable: agnosia, semaphore,
    von Hippel-Lindau disease.

Horseshoes

for Douglas Maxwell

It's slipping by, tiny aliquots
of DNA, memory scratched out
like an old 78 RCA recording,
tintinnabular, and rhonchal
as a forty-year smoker.
They play horseshoes, the men
squatting slightly then heaving up the iron
and letting go. One eighty-three-year-old
plants it; it lands partway round the small post.
He waits. You're still up, the aide says loudly.
He lifts the iron again. The idea
of the post and the horseshoe momentarily
escapes him. You're ahead, another man
offers. You can skip your turn.
There was breakfast, or it's almost
breakfast. The sun sits over the post
and the metal is rusty. A bell rings
in the background. It might be
a telephone, it might be a son in California,
a stockbroker wanting to sell AT&T
(it went down for years). Your turn!
someone yells. He crooks his elbow.
The post comes into focus and he throws.
The metal wraps completely around.
You always win, Jessup complains.
You must have been a professional,
the aide says. The sun casts a long
narrow shadow. It might be dinner.
Green beans and a slice of meat.

Sunrise in Virgin Gorda

The sea, almost slate blue, a four-masted schooner
slipping past Tortola. Who's out this early? What crew
would work, and where are they headed
in such a hurry? Next door a baby cries.
I've never been an "early person." Back home
I'm certain my mother's already eaten breakfast

and walked three miles. Last week I was in Peekskill
by eight to cover an office. Nine patients were waiting
at the door. They were there for chemo: a five-minute push,
a thirty-minute drip, a four-hour infusion. It's always like this,
the nurse explained. No matter when I start
they are here before me. The boat pushes

south, each sail taut. Its large sleek hulk
tacks at least ten degrees to port.

Say Yes

If I cut down on fatty foods, lose
fifteen pounds, work out three times
a week, will I avoid a heart attack?

If only every question were that simple.
It's an opportunity to answer unequivocally,
to give patients a sense of purpose

and hope, even if they've always been obese,
refractory to treatment, unable to comply
with a regimen. Still, just to say yes

is palliative, even though they know
the answer isn't accurate. They don't want
to hear statistics and vacillation.

Just to be like the surgeon who says,
It's 100% curable—I got it all, omitting
the possibility that a cell, a micro-

metastasis, may already be elsewhere.
Say yes—a sliver of grace in an
excoriated world. I must try it sometime.

Not God

I thought to delay the answer, camouflage
it, by waiting until he asked another
question. But he prefaced the question with

I know you're not God. This is commonly said
to me, second in frequency only to What
would you do if it was your father, or wife,

etc. I accept this statement of my undeity
to be rhetorical, a mechanism to permit me
to be imprecise, to use phrases like "it depends

upon many factors" and "a range of." But lately
I'm increasingly tempted to say, How do you know
I'm not God? What gives you such certainty?

Do you say this to your lawyer, accountant,
or mother-in-law? And, if I'm not God then why
ask me a question that only God can answer?

II

Banner Hopes

Tel Aviv, Winter 1996

Banner hopes, and the dusk edges along the wall
like ghost beats. Who wants to know? What else
is there to say? Ruminations are molecules
stacked like pie plates in the brain. War,

warlords, terrorists, assassins—word grenades
to disassemble. A boy who's seven,
a girl from New Jersey, an old man
with sixteen grandchildren, and the sallow
face attached to the knapsack filled

with a homemade recipe: butter, bread, salt,
and a thousand nails. What is there to say? Maybe if we kill
his brother the next one will hesitate? His teacher?
His teacher's son and daughter? If we ring
the perimeter with absolute anger?

Don't say this is war! War is (1) open armed conflict
between countries and (2) military operations
as a profession. I am worn out explaining
this, while fragments of mitral valves, gastric

linings, nasal cilia, stain the pavement. I am worn out
hoping, and if I am not here to hope
then the pusillanimous will seethe out
of this corner, and my banner

(which also has no writing) will be shredded.
Maybe if I can diagram it someone else
can carry it. Maybe if my hope is surrounded
by perfect beads, a polymer that soaks up
time, and blood, and misused adjectives.

Maybe if my hope mutates and infects
a little boy before he is told to put
the knapsack on, the soldier who pushes
an old woman down, the journalist
who explains things didactically, the politician

who prevaricates. I would lay it out completely
unfurled, colors and diagrams that would astound
and each one would draw in a lungful
of fresh air, then smile. Let me hold that baby
awhile. I like its sucking sound.

Le Mas du Luberon

I stretch my legs after a midday meal: fresh morels,
a succulent lamb ragout. As the sun slants over the square,
Monsieur Bouchon opens the orange awning.
One could cook bread on the cobblestones, he says.
Across the square the general store lowers its slatted shutters.

At four the local women buy butter, vegetables,
tins of pâté. Where I stay nearby, at Le Mas du Luberon,
the rooms of the ancient farmhouse are filled with exquisite
antiques. The owner, a dealer in Paris, rents it in July
to those of us who seek reprieve in the countryside.

I cross miles of back roads of Provence by bike. I see farmers
bent over small plots of cucumbers, women fattening geese.
Today I stop for a dusty train headed east to Alsace,
then Tuscany, a farmer who pulls up next to me explains.
His name is Horowitz. That's impossible, I suggest. No, it's true,

he tells me. I discovered this only ten years ago. When I was
    five
I was taken to the square. All my friends were there at the
    depot,
each with a small suitcase. Behind the general store my parents
push me into the arms of a farmer, Colvert. I'm brought here.
I study in a nunnery. I go through catechism. I marry,

have five children, run the farm. What about your wife, your
    children?
I ask. My parents boarded a train like that, he said, pointing
    east.
We owned an elegant farmhouse near town. They collected
    antiques.
I'm a farmer. I grow sweet corn and delicate peppers.
My name is Horowitz, Abram Horowitz of Luberon.

19332

First at breakfast, now next to me
on the beach in Barbados. Maybe
if I concentrate on the emerald water;
nineteen sailboats in the bay, thirty-three
windsurfers. I stop, realizing the symmetry.
The numbers: a blue black tattoo, so clear

over fifty years later. And, when I talk
to her, she swings the left suntanned forearm
around—numbers in full view. She asks me
what I do—where I live—about my
children. I say: doctor—New York—two.
There's the symmetry again. Such a low

number, meaning she was taken early.
She tells me her age; captured at nineteen,
I calculate. The forearm flashes again. Nineteen
sailboats. She sees me staring. The world
comes full circle, she says, pointing. Everything
has meaning. This number was meant to survive.

Two men behind me playing steel drums . . .

Venetian Glass

The Glass Museum of Murano is fifteen minutes
by boat from Venice. Its most exquisite piece
is a large fifteenth-century bowl. It looks as if
a thin layer of crystalline water
is miraculously held aloft. Here and there
tiny portions are painted with scenes

of a royal event. The delicate features,
the use of gold, citron, and light blue, remind me
of Botticelli. One side of the bowl is missing.
The guide explained that even
the broken fragment would be priceless. Outside,
awaiting the boat, a young Israeli man

was leaning against the piling. He was dark
and thin. His right hand curled up and shook
rhythmically. What? he asked his mother,
as his face contorted in a grimace.
His words coalesced and split apart
like shards. It's your injury, she explained.

The war. What? he asked again,
as saliva ran down his chin. As he turned
to board, I saw a wedge of sun cross
his cheek. His skin was streaked orange, cerise,
and madder red—his blue eyes brushed
with amber and green.

Chimes

It sounded like chimes. How else
would a five-year-old hear an anapestic
beat, Aramaic, with an internal rhyme?

Kaddish de-rabbanan, a prayer for the dead,
an incantation said on the Sabbath
and High Holidays. I knew it by heart—
this sonorous dirge, quick alliteration,
hard-voweled words, and in retrospect,

the first poem I learned. I admit now
I liked it. Early on I was asked
to lead the congregation. I would liken
my voice to a violin, the bowstring

drawing out its three beats, attenuating
the first two, slowing stretching the last
with vibrato. The women would cry. The old men
would wrap themselves tightly in their tallisim.

I did this regularly, and yet, I never understood
the meaning. What was the point? All the prayers
seemed the same in English. God's power, God's
goodness, man's weakness. It was the sound

I loved, church bells on a Sunday morning
in Tuscany, Bloch's cello concerto, second
movement. Even when my father died,
and I was required to say the Kaddish every day

for eleven months, I'd close my eyes.
I am five, listening to its chimes: *b'alma
di v'ra khir'utei, v'yamlikh malkhutei.*

The Day Stalin Died

I leaned my weight against the mower:
wooden wheels, thin metal blades in need
of sharpening. Earlier in the day
I was in a spelling bee—stumped
on appetite—forgetting the second *p*.
After school Kenny Teuton asked me
if it's true that Jews drink blood

on holidays. I looked at his wide face,
large spaces between his teeth. Had he
not asked so innocently, I would have
smashed his lower lip, just like I did
to Howard Breckinridge on Lindbergh Street.
Dinner on Thursday was always string beans
and lamb chops. Grandma Katy was there.

She baked potatoes with fried chicken skins
mashed inside. Sunday we'd be visiting
Grandpa Max at the cemetery. I'd stolen
a pail of nails and two wagonloads of lumber
from Woodfield Road for Stephen.
Miriam was on the phone with Rhoda
Stopnick. I turned the Dumont on.

Edward R. Murrow was talking
with a cigarette dangling from his mouth.
I heard my father come home. I was supposed
to be doing homework. Instead,
I was reading *Freddie the Pig*. Freddie
had just unionized all the animals
and was planning a nonviolent protest in town.

The Steam Bath

My younger brother stood in the center
of the huge tiled room—the Turkish
steam bath at Brighton Beach. He was
thin and white as an oyster shell,
surrounded by bulbous naked men
dripping puddles of sweat.
I can't breathe, he cried. It's good for you,
my father said, as my brother bolted
for the door.

Now I wonder how my father knew
it's true, that breathing in the viscous heat
is healthful. So much of childhood
is offered in rote: this is good,
this isn't. So little room
for reflex. And yet at the moment of birth
the diaphragm descends. A breath's
drawn in. A breath's pushed out.

Pelicans

One pelican after another dives
next to me. I have quietly floated
at the inlet of Mahoe Bay until
they were used to me. I take a small
sip of water without disturbing them.

They are like children. They trust
so easily. Then a hunter comes along
and clubs a seal pup, a man entices
a young girl into his car, a woman beats
her four-year-old repeatedly, with

a shoe heel, a leather strap, a small
brass buckle. It wells up like a ball inside,
a tumor, so large it may be impossible
to expel. I sit here another hour. One pelican
seems to offer me half his fish.

The King and I

I saw *The King and I* on an overseas flight.
I'd forgotten that Yul Brynner dies in the end.
My family constantly tells me I block out

unhappy events. Just yesterday my sister reminded me
of two serious accidents. At age nine I fractured my arm
riding my bike down my grandmother's stoop.

At twelve I was hit by a car and thrown to the ground
unconscious. She says I forget because I'm an optimist.
I remind her of a beating when she was eight

and I was five. It was in the kitchen, by the yellow
refrigerator. It wasn't with the brass buckle
on the brown leather strap kept in the hallway closet.

This time it was a shoe, blue, with a long thin heel
and metal tip. The skin on my right forearm broke
in three places. My sister denies it completely.

Shoe Box

Sooner or later it returns to
　　my cards, fastidiously kept,
age five to fifteen, five-cent packs
　　with flat pink bubble gum,
won with dexterity, two and a half flips
　　from the hip, a leaner, a used
Mickey Mantle for Mel Ott,
　　a mint Honus Wagner today
worth $600,000, thrown away,
　　discarded by my mother
when we moved to Ocean Parkway,
　　apartment 6F with a terrace,
rear room facing the alley, because
　　a man offered my father $46,000
for our house, a size 8½ double E
　　shoe box, 2,000 cards cataloged
ten years, and now I tell my wife, my
　　two children, my dog, my poet
friend who plays left field, my
　　analyst, that my childhood
vanished in that box.

III

Green Dust

An old man arcs his slim wooden fishing pole.
A boy skims a stone across the water. I am

seven thousand miles from home. In this river town
south of St. Petersburg, tiny wooden shacks

are capped with tin roofs. A sallow-skinned man
in coarse woolen slacks sells cigarettes, homemade

vodka, soggy tomatoes. A woman wearing
a yellow babushka scrapes gristle from the bone.

This could have been me. My father's mother
died of typhus when he was two. He left school

at age eleven. There's a picture of him, age
fifteen, slender and sinewy, dark eyes glistening

as if dotted with iron ore. As a young boy
I worked in his store in lower Manhattan.

At the end of the day he spread a thin layer
of green dust on the old wooden floor. He swept

in hard even strokes until the oak glowed
like winter moonlight on a Russian lake.

The Green Dodge

I was about to call my father. I know
it's impossible—he died ten and a half years
ago, but I almost picked up the phone.
I stood up and looked out the window
of my study. It was the first sunny day
in weeks. The lake edged over its bank
and the ice had shiny circular pockets
as if someone had scattered its surface
with silver dollars. We first came here
in his Dodge, a sleek green car
with an oversized motor that made the rear end
fishtail in bad weather. The house is too isolated,
he said, too big a financial risk. The last time
he visited he wore his blue running suit
with a red and white vertical stripe.
He'd been losing weight again and refused
further chemo. I helped him up
to look out the window. It was early April.
A late freeze flounced the shoreline
with thin ripples of ice. I never noticed before—
it looks like whipped cream, he said. A deer
incautiously stepped off the shore. Its foot nearly
broke through before it quickly leapt back.
My father smiled. I walked him to his chair.

Words

A cynosure of fashion. That's
what he was before the illness.
I like that word, cynosure. Sometimes
I think I've been waiting for the right moment
to use it. My father used long words
and difficult words when he censured
us. Like the time Andy and I
took the tire out and rolled our neighbor
Johnnie inside, an annoying
three-year-old. The tire took off down

the street, crossed in front of a moving
car, and crashed against a tree. Johnnie
was fine, but my father said (and I was five
at the time) our judgment
was derelict, devoid of . . . etc. I loved
the alliteration. He also capitalized
many words to place emphasis
on the first letter. They said
he had melena and
angiodysplasia.

Monday

Miami Beach: Everyone is eighty-two. Fourteen men
walking on the boardwalk look exactly like my father.

It is inauguration day in Washington, Martin Luther King
Day, and back in New York the temperature's

twenty-two. The last time I was here I spent three days
in the ICU, my father on a cardiac monitor, IVs

supporting his pressure. I am attending a conference
on memory. An anthropologist speaks about anti-

aesthetics in the museum world. A curator talks about
the controversy surrounding the installation of the cattle car

in the Holocaust Museum, how a survivor on the board
refused to step into the building if she was required

to walk through. I am thinking about Mr. Vallone.
The pain in his hip has increased again and the PSA

levels are higher. I am thinking about my father returning
three months later jaundiced, about his sister who said

I was criminal to treat him, about the day he had gram-negative
sepsis, the walk we took in Belle Harbor after

he responded. A man going by has the same mustache.
My father asked me to grow a beard. I kept it six years

after he died, and then it was gray, and my son married.
I'm trying to think of a treatment for Mr. Vallone.

My Father's Shadow

I am my father's shadow, faint and elliptical
on a dusty road. I am the shadow of the grandfather
I never knew, except from a photo—gray long coat,
thick mustache. I don't speak their languages,
their dialects; they crisscrossed so many borders.
I don't know any of them: the bent-over tailors,
penniless students, bearded merchants, thin-boned
housewives, ghostly Jews. They are nothing now
but beads of chromosomes, a piece here and there,
one with diabetes, another perhaps
with coronary artery disease, and another
with curiosity as sharp as a tiger's tooth.
I am number one-sixty, or thereabout. My son
is as thick as a tree, my daughter lighter
than sunshine. They are number one-sixty-one,
and unto them I lay down my shadow.
It barely shimmers in the autumn breeze.

Butterfly

for Sarena

I desire to say something explicit.
    A door will open. A caterpillar
will pass through this light and transform
    itself into a butterfly. I am missing
a noun. I am thinking about a tree
    with thick green leaves as broad
as an idea. I am thinking incrementally
    that the light and the door
are photons, that the caterpillar
    is a centipede of thoughts.

I desire a past with doors that open
    internally. I think of it as a question
of responsibility, as layers of history,
    as accumulated neurons.
I was named for a man who died in '35.
    My daughter is named for the tree,
the open door. A thought enters
    as a scintilla of light. It leaves
like a butterfly, a beautiful shiny butterfly.
    Am I explicit?

My Daughter Graduated from Law School Today

I pulled out an old photo. This is July
in St. Louis. She's wearing
her Raggedy Ann dress and her mother's

blue straw hat. Each time I aimed the camera
she looked away, so I lay back and watched
the sun creep over the asphalt roof

and dip beneath its peak. Just as I turned,
I caught the last light as it filtered through the hat
across her cheeks. Her eyes were dark

and translucent as sorrel agates, and her chin
tilted forward as if to contest the axis
of the earth. She was two years old.

Breathing-Spoons

Breathing-spoons. That's what my grandmother
called them—wooden ladles she dipped into
the thick vegetable soup. Not as thick as your wrist,
I teased. And I could tease her. I could say her potato salad
was sour, the coleslaw was stringy, that she always

grabbed my food away before I finished. I could tease her,
even when she touched my hand and said, You forgot
your old grandmother. And you're getting a little senile,
I'd joke. But it was true. She forgot her second son's name,
Joe, who had died fifteen years earlier. And it was true

her wrists were thick. I only lied about the potato salad.
It was warm and delicate with sprigs of fresh parsley.
Today, my daughter straightens my bow tie just before
we start down the aisle. She smiles. I cover her face
with a veil. You're so elegant, she says.

IV

*Anyway**

A week before I was admitted here
I was in the Metropolitan Museum. I was obliged
to go—you know, a fund-raiser
for the local arts council. I've been active
for years. They support amateur theater
at the library. I once thought of playwriting,
but I have no talent. Anyway,
there was a painting by Pontormo
that was transfixing. I've never responded like that
before—not to Rembrandt, Titian, or even
van Gogh. He was a solitary boy with one eye
shifted slightly. Strabismus, right?
Anyway, he was so sad, about thirteen,
dressed in blue velvet and lace. Something
troubled him deeply and he was trying
so hard to be grown-up as if too much
was expected of him. Anyway, I was still nauseated
from the chemo and I was thinking
about that painting when Carol
walked by.

Cricket[*]

They keep this place so clean. It's
Hector, a slight elderly Hispanic man
who mops here twice a day. Twice a week
he uses an industrial polisher. We barely
converse. Today I said, Hector,
I hear a cricket in this room. He was mortified
and began to search behind the radiator
and under the bed until I was able to explain
I was teasing. I apologized. I told him
how much I rely on him that this room is
meticulous. After three weeks in this hospital
it's almost the only thing I can count on.

Eleventh Floor*

A van near the west parking lot sells bagels,
jelly rolls, hot dogs, and soda. I can't read its sign
from here, but I see a workman holding a can
in one hand and with the other eating food
from a paper wrapper. I don't know why
they design these buildings so high. A conference
on hospital architecture should have been convened
to establish the optimum height. I doubt many
have paid attention to this. What if
a patient is acrophobic? Wouldn't it be better
if one were level with a flowering dogwood,
a Japanese maple? From here I look down
on sunsets. Why the eleventh floor? Admissions
is on the first, radiology the second, surgery the third,
pediatrics the fourth, obstetrics the fifth. Everyone knows
what's in the basement. Perhaps that's why
oncology is so far away.

Apple Cores

Suppose, just suppose, you're shown
an apple core and are asked to describe
its inside, having seen hundreds before
    (they've all been pretty much the same),
but the question put to you,
almost as a matter of life-and-death,
    makes you wary—there may be
an exception, a core unlike any you've ever seen,
yellow and luminescent with garnetlike seeds,
    or no seeds, or no core.
Do you generalize, not having analyzed
the issue, having no statistical data?
    And even if you knew everything
about apple cores, the very latest studies
and their methodology, would you answer
    simply, or would you equivocate,
knowing each word is a shard of glass,
translucent, dazzling, and dangerous?

Calcium

"Sort it out, folks, simplify. Now imagine yourself
a calcium ion." Each professor had his own style.
I curiously watched Joe Aleti squint his eyes shut
as if picturing himself a molecule. He so wanted
to be a physician he was willing to imagine himself
almost anything, even a twelve-membered carbon ring.
I found this lecturer's homespun style corny
and pretentious. "Now suppose too many of you

are crowded in a room and we change the acid base to . . ."
The point of course was to have us understand
calcium metabolism. Later, I was to impart this much differently,
more mechanistic and didactic, certain
they would remember it better. But now as I look back
some thirty years I wonder who had the greater impact.
Sometimes I still see Joe Aleti twisting
his arms and torso into a strange and wonderful shape.

Pinguid

I came across this word unexpectedly.
It means fatty, greasy, unctuous—I can't say exactly
since I've not seen it before. That's the beauty
of words—such surprise and variation, each synonym
with a slightly different meaning. I think of unctuous
as a wormy, mealymouthed flatterer; greasy, a male:
disingenuous, pomaded, cigarette dangling
from mouth. It's in these nuances that we position
ourselves. Today, a patient asked me to explain
highly mitotic. It was on her biopsy report. She said
the dictionary described it as cell division.
It doesn't mean exactly that, I said. Then what?
she asked. Words sometimes take on special meanings,
I explained. It's dependent on the context, the background
of the person using it. So what does it mean then?
she pressed again. I thought for a second about how
I might answer, craft an accurate explanation,
tinge the meaning with ambiguity, how it might slip
along the surface, viscous and opaque, pinguid and smooth.

A Half Billion—More or Less

I asked an agricultural economist how
we would feed eight billion by the year
2050. Not to worry, he said. Now
data suggest there will be a half billion fewer:
war, lower birthrate, the spread
of AIDS. It's indecent to count on pestilence,
I suggested. That's naive, he retorted. I've led
an international conference.
We don't rely on a specific disease
or maelstrom. We factor in relative rates
and trends based on hundreds of events. Please
explain then, I argued, how your hypothesis accommodates
global warming, the end of Communism,
a new bubonic plague, the greenhouse effect?
Overpopulation control, he said, is a euphemism
for what we experts call coercive correct-
ions. And it isn't measured by a mere
half billion. Assuming continued improvement
in farm yield, genetically engineered
meat, family size reduction of sixteen percent,
it won't occur until 2304,
at a population of twenty billion—more
or less.

Recidivism

Habitual or chronic relapse—nowadays it primarily refers
to an inability to maintain weight loss. It's a rarefied term
relegated to scientific texts on nutrition. This points to the
    difficulty
of our language, rife with insider words, ambiguous meanings,
and silent *e*'s. Note that the preceding word in the dictionary is
    recherché.
We've even appropriated gratuitous accents from French.
Some languages such as Hebrew are clear and easy to read. The
    Psalms
are lucid and melodic after three thousand years. In contrast,
    try *Beowulf,*
King Lear, or Allen Ginsberg. Recidivism—reductive and
    malaprop
as pleurisy and chronic fatigue; awkward, syncretic, and tetra-
syllabic. Yet there it is, incestuous shibboleth, hieroglyphic
gnome, a nosocomial word parasite. But I take heart.
It will only exist in a microsecond of mumblings of this post-
pithecanthropine species, except perhaps in Liverpool and
    Biloxi,
where dialect has mutated along its own cavernous course.

The Rainy Season

It's the rainy season in Virgin Gorda
just after the hurricanes. I'm checking
the cisterns for sediment. I'm checking

the foundation for cracks. The soil
has eroded again. The bougainvillea
is anemic but survives. I will

fix the screens, repaint the siding
as I did last year. I like to rebuild.
Thirty years ago I dissected a cadaver.

I named him Melvin. We all chose names,
as we moved backward, unraveling
a human being, undoing creation.

Like Me

When I was two, my doctor
had a large house
on Cortelyou Road. The exam room
smelled like a dead frog
and my temperature was taken
rectally. By age five
I was injected with tetracycline
monthly
by Dr. Ryan. He later died

of lung cancer. Who influenced me
the most? a medical school
interviewer asked. Thirty years later
I still don't know. Today
a sixteen-year-old girl said
she'd like to be
just like me, as I pushed
her third course
of chemotherapy.

Repetition

I see
the bleak parakeet dancing
in the cage, the spores multiplying
with mocking smiles. This isn't

a dream.
This is a cross-reference
in my brain, something a little Valium
will extract. I constantly see things

this way,
dark and dangled, cankerous
and pustular. It is the repetition. It must be.
After all, when I was five

the world
looked green from behind my handlebars.
Later, I dated a girl with wonderful ankles.
I drew favorable analogies.

Alas,
I was an optimist before I saw dustbins
fill with decomposed corpuscles, tume-
faction break the bone,

shrivel
the skin, a gasping plasmodium
wrinkle in bed. All this senselessness—
and then again, and again.

Fifth Finger

A tissue slide on the microscope
flips upside down as if to reverse
its diagnosis. My golf ball sits on the tee
like the lumpectomies I infused
with isotope.

It is twenty-eight years ago. John Lennon's
photo is stapled in my research book.
Abe Janower picks his teeth with a needle
used to inject the mice. I killed them,
forty-two

thousand in all. With my right hand
I tightly pinched the skin on the back,
pressed its belly on a board,
quickly looping the tail in my
fifth finger.

Then with left thumb and index finger
behind the head, I stretched its neck.
In room 5D19, building 37, the National
Cancer Institute, I became expert
at this.

What I Am

You ask me how I know.
    It's hard to say. It's not
something I could easily
    teach, like palpation
of an enlarged liver.

I couldn't describe it
    with precision, e.g.,
sixth-nerve palsy, the sound
    of mitral stenosis. Still,
after twenty years

it's unmistakable. A fine tremor
    of his eyebrow,
the skin below his chin
    like paper-mache,
the way his shoulder

tilts back to the right.
    He has less than
a few months to live. I can't say
    it's vascular,
or neurologic, or even

cancer, which I see
    every day. I only know
it's progressive
    and irreversible. It's
what I am proficient at.